Electric Pressure Cooker

The Best 99 Recipes of Your Favorite Quick and Easy Instant Pot Cookbook.

Table of Contents

Introduction

Do you absolutely love cooking? Are you looking for ways by which you can make some of the finest and the most delicious breakfast, lunch and dinner which will leave everyone happy? Here in this book, we will talk of some of the easiest pot recipes which can be made easily and quickly.

When it comes to recipes, it is important to list both the ingredients and the apt working method as well. Until and unless, the instructions are clear, it won't really be easy for you to come up with great meals. We understand this point well and this is why we have made it a point to bring to you 99 of the healthiest and the most complete recipes.

The book will provide you with a list of ingredients that you will need, and provide you easy to follow directions. Your family and friends will think you have transformed into a gourmet cook, only you will know what little time you spent.

The next hurdle a lot of people face is cooking it. We do realize that not all of us are proficient in the art of cooking and so it becomes important to understand as to how to cook the meals precisely. Once again, this well-formulated book will come to your rescue as you will be able to find some of the most amazing and simple recipes that can be made in no time.

With these recipes, even if you are not a pro at cooking, you will be able to make some of the most delicious dishes which will help you have a satiating meal. With these detailed recipes, you do not need any other instructions and regardless of your cooking skills, you will be able to make each of these recipes and they will taste absolutely yummy.

So, now is the time to bring to rest all your confusion and hassles pertaining to what you should cook! Let us give you 99 of the best and quick recipes you could ask for. You can slowly try your hand at each one of them and be sure to entertain your guests and the compliments for your smart and incredibly delicious cooking are not going to stop anytime soon.

All you need to do is make sure that you adhere to the details which we will list and your compliments as a pro chef is sure to go on endlessly and people will love to eat what you cook.

So, let us get started on our journey of having a healthy start to the day with the finest breakfast meals made with ease. You can, of course, tweak the meals based on your own preferences and needs.

Pressure Cooker Chilled Fruit Soup

Ingredients:

- 1 tbsp of powdered sugar
- 2 peaches (remove the pit)
- ½ cantaloupes
- 8 oz of Greek yogurt
- 16 oz of fresh pineapple juice
- 1 large sized orange (cut it in two halves each)
- 1 tbsp of chia seeds
- ½ tsp of vanilla

Directions:

1. Take the prepared fruit having the pineapple juice
2. Add it to the pressure cooker tactfully.
3. Put the pressure to HP for the next 5 minutes and release it quickly after that.
4. Now, pour it in a blender after the time is up and puree it until the texture becomes smooth.
5. Pour it using a strainer.

6. Let it cool to room temperature and now add vanilla, powdered sugar and some Greek yogurt.

7. Whisk to mix thoroughly.

8. Chill and serve with chia seeds for best results.

Smoky Ham Hock with Pinto Bean Soup

Ingredients:

- A few bay leaves

- 2 cups of Pinto beans

- 1 smoked ham hock

- 1 tsp of cumin powder

- 6 crushed garlic cloves

- 1 onion

- Cilantro and minced tomatoes (for garnishing)

- 1 pinch of oregano

- 5 cups of unsalted chicken stock

- Salt and pepper

Directions:

1. Start by taking the lid off from the pressure cooker and adding all the above-mentioned ingredients to it.

2. Now, you can set the cooker and let it be at HP (high pressure) for 50 minutes.

3. Lastly, season it with some salt and pepper.

4. Garnish it and serve.

Cinnamon Apple Steel Cut Oats

Ingredients:

- 1 large peeled apple
- 1 cup of steel cut oats
- 1 tbsp of butter
- 2 tbsp of sugar (brown)
- 3 ½ cups of water
- 1 ½ tsp of ground cinnamon
- ¼ tsp of salt

Directions:

1. Start by taking the pressure cooking pot and add butter to it. After the butter has been melted, add oats and toast

2. Mix it for another 3 minutes.

3. Now, add apples, cinnamon, water together. Sprinkle some brown sugar along with salt.

4. Set pressure to high and cook it for 10 minutes

5. Use "natural press release" for the next 10 minutes and follow it with quick pressure release.

6. After the valve drops, remove the lid and stir the oats. Cover and let it sit for 5 or 10 minutes until oats thicken.

7. Add some nuts, milk and brown sugar to give it a finished touch.

Pressure Cooker Chicken Noodle Soup

Ingredients:

- 4 large carrots

- 2 cups of diced chicken

- 6 cups of chicken stock

- 1 onion (diced)

- Egg noodles

- 1 diced celery rib

- 1 tbsp of butter

- Salt and pepper

Directions:

1. Take the lid off from the pressure pot and select sauté mode before adding anything.

2. When the butter has been melted, add some onion and cook it for 1 to 2 minutes.

3. Now, you can add carrots and celery as well. Let them sauté for nearly 5 minutes.

4. This would be your cue to add chicken stock and chicken.

5. Place the pot to HP and set the timer for 5 minutes.

6. After that wait for another 5 minutes for a quick pressure release.

7. Add required salt and pepper.

8. Serve along with prepared noodles.

Pressure Cooker Breakfast Quinoa

Ingredients:

- 2 tbsp of maple syrup

- ½ tsp of vanilla

- 2 ¼ cups of water

- 1 ½ cups of well-rinsed quinoa

- ¼ tsp of ground cinnamon

Directions:

1. Take the pressure cooking pot off-lit and add quinoa, vanilla, cinnamon, water, salt and a required quantity of maple syrup to it.

2. Now, set it to HP and leave it for 1 minute to cook.

3. After that, wait for another 10 minutes and select the "quick pressure release".

4. Water the valve drops, remove the lid while tilting it away.

5. Lastly, fluff the quinoa and serve with berries and milk for the most delicious result.

Instant Pot Minestrone Soup

Ingredients:

- 1 tsp of oregano
- 3 garlic cloves
- 2 tbsp of olive oil
- 1 onion
- 1 carrot
- 2 celery stalks
- 1 tsp of dried basil
- 4 cups of vegetable/bone broth
- 28 oz of canned tomatoes
- 1 bay leaf
- ½ cup of spinach
- 2 tbsp of fresh pesto
- 1 cup of elbow pasta
- 15 oz of cannelloni beans
- 1/3 cup of grated parmesan cheese
- Salt and pepper

Directions:

1. Start by setting the Instant Pot to sauté mode.

2. Add onion, carrot, garlic, celery, and olive oil. Mix it.

3. Blend canned tomatoes in a food processor and dice them.

4. Now, add tomatoes, spinach, pasta, bay leaf, and bone broth to the mix.

5. Set it at HP for the next 6 minutes.

6. Let it fit for the next 2 minutes.

7. Add salt and pepper and serve it with grated cheese and pesto.

Paleo Banana Bread

Ingredients:

- 1/3 cup butter

- 1 cup coconut sugar

- 1 tsp of vanilla essence

- 2 ripe and mashed bananas

- 1 cup of flour

- 1 egg

- 1 tsp of baking powder

- ½ tsp of baking soda

- 1 tsp of cream of tartar

- 1/3 cup of cashew or coconut milk

- Pinch of salt

Directions:

1. Take a small bowl and mix milk and cream of tartar together to form buttermilk.

2. Now, add egg, vanilla, butter and sugar together. Mix it.

3. Add bananas (mashed) to the mix.

4. Take a separate bowl and mix flour, baking soda, baking powder and salt.

5. Add this mix to the wet ingredients.

6. Add the buttermilk to the mix.

7. Cover the mix with a foil.

8. Now, add 2 cups of water to the pot and set the metal trivet track.

9. Put the batter onto the trivet. Close the pot and set its knob to sealing. Let it stay on the manual mode for the next 30 minutes. After while, the instant pot will release the pressure. Once it is cooled down, place it in the refrigerator overnight for best results.

Instant Pot Applesauce

Ingredients:

- 10-12 diced apples

- ½ cup of apple juice

Directions:

1. Open the Instant Pot and placed the diced apple slices in the inner part.

2. Add some apple juice to it.

3. Cut a parchment paper and place it over the diced slices.

4. After covering the lid, set it to "sealing".

5. Select the Manual setting and add cooking time to 10 minutes.

6. Let the pressure release naturally.

7. Uncover the parchment paper.

8. Blend it until it would become smooth and refined.

Pressure Cooker Baked Apples

Ingredients:

- 5-7 apples
- 1 cup of red wine
- ¼ cup of raisins
- ½ cup of raw sugar
- 1 tsp of cinnamon powder

Directions:

1. Start by placing the apples at the base.
2. Sprinkle the raisins and add sugar and cinnamon powder. Pour some wine as well.
3. Close the lid and cook it for next the 10 minutes at HP (high pressure).
4. Open it with the natural release pressure and let it calm for another 10 minutes.
5. Serve it hot. You can add the cooking liquid to make it more moist and warm.

Creamy Potato Soup with Kale

Ingredients:

- 1 diced onion
- 2 cloves of garlic
- 1 carrot
- 2 diced celery
- ½ tsp of celery salt
- 4 cups of diced potatoes
- ½ cup of frozen corn
- 1 cup of chopped kale
- 3 cups of vegetable broth
- ¼ cup of coconut milk

Directions:

1. Start by taking onion and garlic together and sauté them.

2. Now, add carrots and chopped celery and sauté it for the next 3-4 minutes. Add some water, if needed.

3. Add the potatoes, vegetable broth, salt and pepper to the mixture.

4. Reduce the heat to low and let it simmer for 10-15 minutes.

5. Use an immersion blender to create a thick and creamy base for the soup.

6. Add kale and corn and stir the mixture

7. Turn the heat off and add coconut milk to it.

8. Serve it hot.

Rice Burrito Bowl With Black Beans And Chicken

Ingredients:

- 1 boneless chicken breast

- 1 tbsp of olive oil

- 1 onion

- 1 green bell pepper

- 1 cup dried beans (soaked overnight)

- 1 tsp salt

- 2 cups water

- 1 tsp pepper

- 1 tsp of cumin powder

- 1 tsp marjoram

- 1 bay leaf

- 1 tsp garlic powder

- 2 cups of shredded lettuce

- 1 tbsp zest

- 250 g of boiled rice

Directions:

1. Start by adding the rice, lime zest and water to the pot.

2. Add the chicken on one side and cook for another 5 minutes.

3. Remove the chicken and add bell pepper, beans, herbs, spices, bay leaf, water, and salt to it. Mix it.

4. Put the chicken breast on the top of the mix. Place the steamer basket on the top of chicken breast.

5. Close the lock of the lid after resting the heat-proof bowl of the rice mix.

6. Cook for the next 6 minutes at HP (high pressure).

7. Let its pressure out in a naturally warm and keep it in the "keep warm" mode.

8. Remove the rice bowl and place it aside. Pour some lime juice over it.

9. Took the steamer basket out and wash it. Place the chicken breast on the plate.

10. Lastly, make a burrito with rice, chicken, bean, and lettuce. Add some sour cream and salsa to it.

Pressure Cooker Corn on the Cob

Ingredients:

- 1 cup of water

- A few tbsp of butter

- Corn on the cob

- A pinch of salt

Directions:

1. Start by cleaning the cork and removing every ounce of husk from it.

2. Cut its stem with a chopping knife before placing it in the pressure cooker.

3. Stand the corn cob at the most suitable angle in such a way that it would get maximum exposure.

4. Add water and kosher salt to it. Place it on HP (High Pressure) mode for the next 3 minutes with "quick release".

5. Remove the lid and take out the corn.

6. Insert corn holders and put pepper, salt and butter to it before taking a bite.

Pressure Cooker Potato Salad

Ingredients:

- 4 eggs

- 1 cup mayonnaise

- 6 medium-sized potatoes

- 1 tbsp of mustard

- 1 tbsp of pickle juice

- 1 cup water

- 2 tbsp of chopped parsley

- Salt and pepper

Directions:

1. Start by placing the steamer basket in the cooker.

2. Add potatoes, eggs and water in it. Place the lid and let it stay at High Pressure for the next 4 minutes.

3. Do a quick pressure release and remove the lid. Take the steamer basket and place the eggs in ice cold water.

4. Take a large bowl and put pickle juice, mustard, onion, parsley, and mayo to it. Add potatoes to the mixture and place the diced eggs as well.

5. Keep stirring the salad and add salt and pepper as per the taste.

Unfried-Refried Beans

Ingredients:

- 1 peeled onion
- 2 tbsp of minced garlic
- 9 cups of vegetable broth (or water)
- 1/8 tsp of cumin
- 1 chopped jalapeno
- 3 cups of dry beans
- Salt and pepper

Directions:

1. Start by placing the ingredients together in a big bowl.
2. Place it in the pressure cooker.
3. Cook it for almost 15-20 minutes on HP (high pressure) and quick release the pressure.
4. If the beans are not soft again, pressure again for some 5-10 minutes.
5. Take it out and add some lime juice, salt and pepper to it before serving.

Instant Pot Hard Boiled Eggs

Ingredients:

- 1 cup water

- Pasture raised eggs

Directions:

1. Start by turning on your Instant Pot and pouring a cup of water in a stainless bowl.

2. Put the bowl in the steam basket.

3. On the top of the basket, place the number of eggs you want.

4. Turn on the lid and put it on the Manual mode.

5. Lock the lid and let it operate for the next 8 minutes.

6. Let the steam out gradually and transfer your eggs to the fridge in order to let them cool down a little before eating.

Vegetable Barley Soup

Ingredients:

- 1 tsp of olive oil
- 2 garlic cloves
- 1 onion
- ½ cup barley
- 1 carrot
- 1 celery stalk
- 1 bay leaf
- A handful of mushrooms
- 1 large potato
- 4 cups of vegetable stock
- 1 tsp of pounded black pepper
- Salt and pepper

Directions:

1. Start by soaking the barley for around 6 hours before you begin.
2. Make sure that the barley is cooked properly. You can also use a sauce pan method to do so.

3. Turn the pressure cooker on and add garlic, onions and celery to sauté it for the next few minutes. Except for parsley, add the remaining ingredients to it.

4. Now, cover the cooker and heat it for at least the next 10 minutes.

5. Release the pressure naturally.

6. Serve the barley vegetable soup by adding salt and pepper to it.

Instant Pot Lentil Tacos

Ingredients:

- 4 oz of tomato sauce

- 2 cups of brown lentils

- 1 tsp, each of onion powder, chili powder, garlic powder, and salt

- 4 cups of water

- ½ tsp of cumin

Directions:

1. Place all the ingredients in the Instant Pot and stir them properly.

2. Seal the pressure cooker and set it on the manual mode.

3. Heat it for some 10-15 minutes.

4. Once it's over, turn off the lid and release the pressure naturally.

5. After opening the lid, carefully stir it.

6. Let it cook for a few minutes before serving it.

Pressure Cooker French Fries

Ingredients:

- 1 tsp of kosher salt

- 16 oz of russet potatoes

- ¼ tsp of baking soda

- Frying oil (do not use olive oil)

- 1 cup cold water

- Salt

Directions:

1. Make sure that the cooker is up and running, and that there is sufficient airspace under the rack.

2. Peel the potatoes and cut them into stick steaks.

3. In the cooker bowl, add a cup of cold water, some salt and baking soda.

4. Now, place the potato slices in the steamer in a single layer.

5. Turn the pressure cooker on HP (high pressure) for 2-3 minutes and set it to quick release.

6. Remove the fries carefully and check for any trace of moisture. Simply dab it away without rinsing or wiping it.

7. Now, put oil at medium high and make sure it is hot enough to fry the potato.

8. Gently place the potato and let it fry until it turns light brown.

9. Take it out gently and place it in a metal rack. Add some salt to it, if you want.

Pressure Cooker Tortellini Soup

Ingredients:

- 1 tbsp dried onions

- 1 tbsp minced garlic

- ½ tbsp of ground pepper

- 1 tbsp of chicken base

- 1 tbsp of dried shallots

- 2 carrots

- ¼ cup of dry vermouth

- 6 ounces of baby spinach

- 6 ounces of cheese tortellini

- 6 cups of chicken stock or broth

- Parmesan cheese

Directions:

1. Add onion, garlic, chicken base, ground pepper, and shallots to the pot.

2. Cut carrots in ¼ inch thick coins and place them in the pot.

3. Place tortellini and add chicken broth and vermouth to it.

4. Set the cooker on High Pressure for 2 minutes with Quick Release.

5. Let the soup cook. Meanwhile, clean spinach leaves.

6. Release the pressure and wait for a few minutes to let the soup settle. Garnish it with parmesan before serving.

Pressure Cooker Oatmeal with Caramelized Apple

Ingredients:

- ¼ tsp of sugar

- 1 cup of milk

- ½ cup of rolled oats

- 1 tbsp butter

- 1 tbsp of Torani syrup

- 1 cup of cold water

- Apple (for topping)

- Butter

- Salt

Directions:

1. Slice off some apple for topping.

2. Add oats, sugar and salt to the pot.

3. Add all the other ingredients together to the pot and thoroughly mix it together.

4. Cook it for the next 2-3 minutes by keeping it HP (High Pressure) and the Quick Pressure Release feature.

5. Meanwhile, heat the apples and sauté them until they are soft. You can also add some butter and Torani syrup to them.

6. Adding a pinch of brown sugar and butter to the apples. Keep heating them until they turn brown.

7. Release the steam and stir the oatmeal before serving it into bowls.

8. Top them with caramelized apples to add a refined appeal to your recipe.

Pressure Cooker Artichokes with Dip

Ingredients:

- 1 cup of cold water
- Lemon slices
- 2-3 artichokes
- Garlic lemon mayo dip
- Salt

Directions:

1. Start by cutting off the stem of every artichoke to make it sit flat.
2. Furthermore, cut them half through the artichoke heart.
3. Take it off from the top and remove the unwanted hair or the purple leaves.
4. Rinse it carefully under the cold water and clean it thoroughly.
5. Place in on the pot by turning its heat down.
6. Lock the lid and set the pressure at HP (High pressure) for the next 5-6 minutes with quick pressure release.
7. Turn it off when the time is up and take the artichokes away using a thong.

8. Since they are warm, you can easily remove their petals.

9. Serve them with some lemon and garlic mayo dip and enjoy them when they are hot.

Cheesy Potatoes Au Gratin

Ingredients:

- ½ chopped onion
- 1 cup chicken broth
- 2 tbsp of butter
- 6 peeled potatoes
- ½ cup sour cream
- 1 cup bread crumbs
- 3 tbsp butter
- Salt and pepper

Directions:

1. Start by melting the butter and add onions to it. Add chicken broth and some salt and pepper to it.
2. Place the steamer basket in the pot and add some sliced potatoes to it.
3. Let it cook for another 5 minutes on HP (High Pressure).
4. Meanwhile, in a small bowl mix the breadcrumbs and the melted butter.

5. "Quick pressure release" the steam and take the basket out of it.

6. Place the potatoes in a safe dish. Meanwhile, stir cheese and sour cream using the cooking liquid of the pressure cooker.

7. Pour it over the potatoes and mix it with the breadcrumbs. Heat it for another 5 minutes to complete the recipe.

Creamy Cauliflower Soup

Ingredients:

- 1 quart chicken broth
- 1 diced onion
- ½ cup butter
- ¾ cup celery
- 1 cup chopped carrot
- 3 garlic cloves
- 1 tsp parsley
- 1 cauliflower
- 1 cup of milk
- 1 cup of sour cream
- 8 ounces of cheese (grated)
- Chives
- 12 slices of chopped and cooked bacon
- 2 tsp of garlic powder
- Salt and pepper

Directions:

1. Start by melting the butter and put the pot to sauté setting.

2. Add carrot, onion, garlic, and celery to it and cook for 5-6 minutes.

3. When the veggies are tender, add cauliflower, chicken broth and parsley.

4. Lock the pressure cooker and heat it for another 3 minutes at Low Pressure.

5. Meanwhile, melt butter and whisk some flour to form a paste.

6. Add milk to the mixture and continue whisking it.

7. Sprinkle the desired quantity of salt, pepper and garlic powder.

8. Simmer the cooker and add the whisked contents to it.

9. Add cheese and sour cream and let it simmer for another few minutes. Sprinkle the sour with some bacon, chives and extra cheese before serving it hot.

Huevos Rancheros Recipe

Ingredients:

- 3 eggs
- ½ cup of salsa
- Vegetable oil
- Tortilla chips
- Salt and pepper

Directions:

1. Start by mixing the salsa and the ramekin.
2. Crack the eggs and add them to the top of salsa.
3. Use an aluminum foil to cover the ramekin.
4. Now, take away the center prong from the steamer and add a cup of water into it.
5. Put the ramekin on its top and cook it for some 20 minutes under Low Pressure with Quick Pressure Release.
6. Meanwhile, prepare your tortilla chips and garnish them.
7. Turn off the "keep warm" feature and release the steam.

8. Make sure it has the desired texture before serving it with chips.

Mexican Green Rice

Ingredients:

- 1 cup chicken broth
- ½ cup cilantro
- 1 cup uncooked rice
- ¼ cup of green salsa
- ½ avocado
- Salt and pepper

Directions:

1. Start by adding the rice and the broth to the cooker.
2. Stir it thoroughly and lock the lid.
3. Heat it on High Pressure for the next 3 minutes.
4. Let it release the steam naturally and wait for the next 10 minutes. This will let the rice to settle.
5. Let the rice cool for a while.
6. Now, add some salsa, cilantro and avocado to it by adding a little water to the mixture.
7. Blend smoothly and add some sour cream in between. Add salt and pepper as per your requirements.

Pasta with Tuna and Capers

Ingredients:

- 1 clove of garlic
- 1 tbsp olive oil
- 1 tsp of salt
- 2 anchovies
- 16 oz of pasta
- 2 cup tomato puree
- 2 tbsp capers
- 2 cans of Tuna (5.5 oz)

Directions:

1. Add garlic, oil and anchovies and sauté them until they turn golden brown.
2. Now, add some puree and salt to the mix.
3. Add pasta and tuna and start stirring it evenly.
4. Pour enough water to cover. Lock the lid and turn on the heat.
5. Cook it under low pressure for the next 3 minutes.
6. When the time is up, take the mixture out and sprinkle with capers and tuna before serving.

Sweet Potatoes and Black-eyed Peas

Ingredients:

- 8 tbsp of milk
- 3 sweet potatoes (sliced in half)
- 1 cup Black-eyed peas
- 1 tbsp olive oil
- 1 onion
- 1 tbsp tomato paste
- 4 cloves of garlic
- ½ tsp of coriander seeds and caraway seeds
- 1 cup water
- 4 oz of spinach
- Salt and pepper

Directions:

1. Start by putting the potatoes in the steamer basket.
2. Toast all the spices for 30 seconds.
3. Add olive oil, garlic and onion, and let it sauté until it becomes tender.
4. Now, place the mix on the black-eyed pea mixture.

5. Close the lid and heat it for 12 minutes under High Pressure.

6. Wait for another ten minutes to the mix to settle.

7. Take the potatoes from the steamer and place it in the mix.

8. Toss salt and mix some spinach in between. Use the residual heat to do this.

9. Serve the potatoes hot with some additional yogurt.

Poached Eggs in Bell Pepper Cup

Ingredients:

- 2 eggs

- 2 bell peppers

- 2 slices of cheese (Gouda or Mozerella)

- 2 slices of wheat bread

For Mock Hollandaise sauce:

- 1 tsp of mustard

- 2/3 cup of mayo

- 3 tbsp of orange juice

- 1 tbsp of vinegar

- 1 tsp of turmeric

- Salt

Directions:

1. Start by making the mock Hollandaise sauce my mixing all the ingredients together until it would result in a smooth mix. Refrigerate it overnight.

2. Add a cup of water to the steamer basket and prepare the pressure cooker.

3. Shape the bell pepper ends to form a cup-shape and break the egg inside it.

4. Cover it with a tin foil and put it in the steamer.

5. Heat the pot on LOW Pressure setting for 4-5 minutes.

6. Release it on the normal mode and take the pepper out.

7. Put some toast, cheese, and other garnishing ingredients on it and serve it with the sauce.

Sweet and Orangey Brussels Sprouts

Ingredients:

- 1 tsp orange zest

- 1 cup Brussels sprouts

- 2 tbsp maple syrup

- ¼ cup of orange juice

- 1 tbsp of buttery spread

- Salt and pepper

Directions:

1. Place all the ingredients in the pot.

2. Cover the lip and put it in the "quick release" mode.

3. If the sprouts are cut in half, set the timer to 3 minutes, else let it heat for 4-5 minutes on the Manual mode.

4. In case if they are not done, you can always cook them for longer.

5. Release the pressure and stir the sprouts together for the sauce to reach evenly.

6. Serve warm and sprinkle salt and pepper.

Green Posole Recipe

Ingredients:

- 1 head of garlic
- 2 x 28 oz. cans of Mexican hominy
- ½ cup of pork
- 15 oz. of chicken broth
- 16 oz. of salsa
- 1 tbsp of chicken base
- 1 tsp of ground cumin
- ½ tsp of pepper
- 1 tsp of ground coriander

Directions:

1. Start by rinsing the canned hominy.
2. Dice the pork evenly. Add broth to the pressure pot and chicken base.
3. Put garlic, salsa, hominy, and meat to it.
4. Heat it for 10 minutes at the High Pressure mode using Quick Pressure Release feature.
5. Add ground cumin and coriander to it and sprinkle enough pepper before serving.

6. Garnish it with cheese while serving hot.

Easy Pot Mushroom Soup

Ingredients:

- 8 oz. white mushrooms
- ¼ cup of milk
- 2 tbsp of virgin oil
- 2 cups of water
- ¼ cup of chicken broth
- 4 tbsp butter
- 4 tbsp flour

Directions:

1. Add oil and sliced mushrooms to the pot to sauté them until they become tender and darker.
2. Add chicken broth to the mix.
3. Put it to the Pressurize mode and set it to quick release feature. Drain the mushrooms while saving the broth.
4. Place the mushrooms back in the pot. Add butter to it and let them simmer.
5. Add flour to the mix and stir it gently.
6. Lastly, add the mushroom broth and let it all dissolve to give a smooth texture.

7. Whisk it for another 8 minutes and add milk to it to complete the recipe.

Wheat Berry Salad

Ingredients:

- 1 cup wheat berries
- 2 cups water
- 3 tbsp oil
- ¼ cup vinegar
- 1 cup sliced onion
- ½ cup dried apricots
- 1 cup dried blueberries
- ½ cup roasted almonds
- 2 tbsp mustard
- 2 tbsp of parsley
- Salt and pcpper

Directions:

1. The night before, rinse the berries and keep them soaked overnight.
2. The next day, start by placing the berries in the instant pot.
3. Heat it for 15-20 minutes on the Manual mode. When it is done, rinse the cold water.

4. Meanwhile, mix mustard, vinegar, salt and pepper together. Add some onion, apricots, almonds, parsley, and blueberries to it.

5. Mix white berries to the mix and let it stay for a few minutes.

6. Refrigerate it for a few hours and garnish it with parsley before serving.

Mediterranean Tuna Noodles

Ingredients:

- 1 cup of water
- 1 tbsp of oil
- 8 ounces of egg noodles
- ½ cup chopped onion
- 7 oz of marinated artichokes
- A can of tuna
- A can of diced tomatoes
- Cheese and parsley (for garnishing)
- Salt and pepper

Directions:

1. Start by placing the oil and onion in the pot and sauté them for the next 2 minutes.
2. Now, add tomatoes, noodles, water, salt and pepper to it.
3. Heat it for the next 10 minutes and release the pressure value.
4. After when the time is up, turn off the warm setting.

5. Add artichoke and tuna to the mix and heat it for the next 4-5 minutes again.

6. Serve it hot by sprinkling some cheese and parsley on it.

Pressure Cooker BBQ Chicken

Ingredients:

- 2 Pounds boneless, skinless chicken thigh's

- 1 Onion minced

- ¾ Cup Chili sauce

- ½ Cup Water

- 2 Tbs. Apple cider vinegar

- ½ Tsp. Salt

- Dash black pepper

Directions:

1. Set pressure cooker on medium and cook chicken until lightly browned, 2-3 minutes per side.

2. Sprinkle with salt and pepper

3. Combine chili sauce, water, onion, and vinegar in a bowl and pour over chicken

4. Cover cooker and cook 15-20 minutes

5. Release with natural method

Pressure Cooker Beef & Rice

Ingredients:

- 2-3 pound chuck roast cut into strips

- 1 cup brown rice

- 3 cups beef broth

- 1 bell pepper chopped

- 1 tbs olive oil

- 1 tsp salt

- ½ tsp pepper

Directions:

1. Put olive oil in cooker and turn on high

2. Add beef and cook 3 minutes

3. Add broth, rice, and pepper

4. Add salt and pepper

5. Cook on high 20 minutes

6. Use slow release method

7. Stir and let stand 5 minutes

Pressure Cooker Sweet & Sour Chicken

Ingredients:

- 3 chicken breast, cut into strips

- 1 tbs olive oil

- ½ cup Heinz 57

- ½ cup apricot preserves

Directions:

1. Put olive oil and chicken in cooker

2. Heat on high for 5 minutes

3. Add Heinz and preserves

4. Cook on high for 15 minutes

Pressure Cooker Tuna Casserole

Ingredients:

- 1 cup tuna packed in water
- 2 cans cream of mushroom soup (fat-free)
- 1 can peas
- ¾ cup chicken broth
- 1 16 ounce package egg noodles
- ½ cup shredded cheese

Directions:

1. Put broth and soup in pot and turn to high
2. Add tuna and peas
3. Cook on high for 2 minutes
4. Add noodles and cook on high for 15 minutes
5. Use quick release method, and stir

Pressure Cooker Beef Stew

Ingredients:

- 2 pounds stew meat
- 4 russet potatoes, peeled and cute into quarters
- 3 carrots, peeled and cut
- 1 large onion cut into quarters
- 2 packets stewed seasoning mix
- 1 tbs olive oil
- 4 cups beef broth

Directions:

1. Put olive oil in pot, add meat
2. Cook on high for 5 minutes
3. Add potatoes, carrots, and onion
4. Add beef broth
5. Stir in seasoning mix
6. Cook on high 20 minutes
7. Use slow release method

Pressure Cooker Sweet & Sour Chicken

Ingredients:

- 3 boneless skinless chicken breast, cut into strips
- 1 tbs olive oil
- ¼ cup BBQ sauce
- ¼ cup lemon juice
- 1 tsp brown mustard
- ¼ cup hot sauce (or mild)
- ½ cup apricot preserves

Directions:

1. Select bowl that fits in cooker
2. Place bowl in pot, and oil and heat on high
3. Add chicken and cook 2 minutes
4. Add bbq sauce, juice, mustard and hot sauce
5. Add preserves and stir
6. Cook on high 15 minutes
7. Use slow release method, and stir

Pressure Cooker Turkey & Dressing

Ingredients:

- 2 pounds boneless turkey breast cut into large strips
- 2 tbs olive oil
- ¼ cup margarine
- 1 24 ounces package stuffing mix
- 6 cups chicken broth
- 1 onion chopped
- 2 stalks celery chopped
- 1 tsp salt
- ½ tsp pepper

Directions:

1. Put olive oil in cooker, add turkey breast and cook 10 minutes
2. Add margarine, celery, onion, salt & pepper
3. Pour in chicken broth
4. Add stuffing mix and stir
5. Cook on high 15 minutes
6. Use quick release method

7. Fluff with fork

Pressure Cooker Spaghetti Sauce

Ingredients:

- 2 pounds lean ground beef
- 2 tbs olive oil
- 2-1/2 cups stewed tomatoes
- 2 tsp oregano
- 1 small onion minced
- 2 cloves garlic minced
- 3 tbs parmesan cheese

Directions:

1. Put olive oil in cooker, add beef
2. Cook 5 minutes
3. Add onion and garlic
4. Stir in tomatoes and oregano
5. Sprinkle on cheese
6. Cook on high 15 minutes
7. Use slow release method
8. Stir & Serve

Pressure Cooker Pork & Vegetables

Ingredients:

- 2 pounds boneless pork chops cut into strips
- 1 green bell pepper chopped
- 1 red bell pepper chopped
- 1 onion chopped
- 1 can green beans
- 1 can stew tomatoes
- 2 tbs olive oil
- 1 clove garlic minced
- 1 tsp salt
- ½ tsp pepper

Directions:

1. Put olive oil in cooker, and pork
2. Cook 5 minutes
3. Add onion and garlic
4. Stir in tomatoes, beans, and peppers
5. Sprinkle on salt and pepper

6. Cook on high 15 minutes

7. Use quick release method

8. Sprinkle on cheese

9. Cook on high 15 minutes. Use slow release method

Pressure Cooker Vegetarian Chili

Ingredients:

- 2 cans stewed tomatoes
- 1 cup tomato juice
- 1 pack chili seasoning (more to taste)
- 1 can black beans
- 1 can chili beans
- 1 cup cauliflower trimmed
- 1 onion chopped
- 1 bell pepper chopped

Directions:

1. Put tomatoes in cooker, and add juice
2. Sprinkle chili seasoning
3. Add black beans and chili beans
4. Add cauliflower, onion and pepper
5. Stir, and cook on high 15 minutes

Pressure Cooker Sausage Jambalaya

Ingredients:

- 1-1/2 pounds smoked sausage or kielbasa cut into pieces
- 1 can stewed tomatoes
- 1 green bell pepper chopped
- 1 red bell pepper chopped
- 1 1 onion chopped
- 2 russet potatoes cubed
- Zatarain seasoning, or spice seasoning
- 1 tsp pepper
- 1 cup chicken broth

Directions:

1. Put sausage in cooker
2. Add tomatoes , peppers, and onions
3. Add potatoes, soup broth and seasonings
4. Cook on high for 15 minutes
5. Release with slow release method

Pressure Cooker Chicken Potato Stew

Ingredients:

- 1 chicken, cut into pieces
- 1 tomato cut into pieces
- 3 potatoes cut into quarters
- 1 bell pepper
- 1 onion chopped
- 1 cup chicken broth
- 1 clove garlic minced
- 2 cans or 2 cups corn
- Salt and pepper to taste

Directions:

1. Turn cooker to high and add chicken, cook 5 minutes
2. Add tomato, potatoes, pepper, and onion
3. Add broth and garlic
4. Add corn, and salt/pepper if desired
5. Cook on high 20 minutes
6. Use slow release method

7. Debone cooked chicken and stir into stew mix

Pressure Cooker Corn Soup

Ingredients:

- 2 cans whole kernel corn (one 3 cups frozen)
- 1 can fat-free evaporated milk
- 1 8 ounces package fat-free cream cheese
- 3 Tbs corn starch
- ¼ cup margarine
- ½ cup Swiss or provolone cheese

Directions:

1. Cooker to medium, and add margarine
2. Put cream cheese and butter in, let cook for 1 minute
3. Add milk and cornstarch, stir
4. Cook on medium 15 minutes
5. Use slow release method
6. Add salt and pepper to taste

Pressure Cooker White Chili

Ingredients:

- 4 boneless skinless chicken breasts, cut into small pieces
- 1 can stewed tomatoes
- 1-1/2 cup tomato juice
- 1 can chili beans
- 1 onion chopped
- 1 cup cauliflower chopped
- 1 cup water
- 1 pack chili seasoning

Directions:

1. Put chicken in cooker, add tomatoes, and juice
2. Add beans, seasoning, onion, and cauliflower
3. Add water and stir
4. Cook on high 20 minutes
5. Use slow release method
6. Stir well before serving

Pressure Cooker Chicken Dumplings

Ingredients:

- 4 boneless skinless chicken breasts cut into pieces
- 1 tbs olive oil
- 4 cups chicken broth
- 2 cans fat-free cream of chicken soup
- 1 can refrigerated biscuits, 8-10 count, broke into pieces
- Salt & pepper to taste

Directions:

1. Turn cooker to high and put in olive oil
2. Add chicken and cook 5 minutes
3. Add broth, and soup, stir
4. Add biscuit dough pieces
5. Cook on high 15 minutes
6. Use slow release method
7. Salt and pepper to taste

Pressure Cooker Southwestern Beef

Ingredients:

- 2 pounds round steak cut into strips
- 2 tbs olive oil
- 1 tsp red pepper
- 1 tsp salt
- ½ tsp black pepper
- 3 russet potatoes cubed and peeled
- 2 onions, chopped
- 1 red, 1 green, and 1 yellow bell pepper chopped
- ¾ cup beef broth

Directions:

1. Put live oil in cooker, add meat and cook for 5 minutes
2. Add onions and peppers, stir
3. Add broth and potatoes
4. Add salt and peppers
5. Cook on high 15 minutes
6. Use slow release method

Pressure Cooker Turkey & Noodles

Ingredients:

- 2 pounds boneless skinless turkey breast
- 4 cups chicken broth
- 1 24 ounce package egg noodles
- 1 can fat-free cream of mushroom soup
- 1 cup or 1 can sweet peas
- 1 tsp salt
- ½ tsp pepper

Directions:

1. Place turkey in cooker and cook 5 minutes
2. Add broth and noodles
3. Add soup and peas
4. Add salt and pepper
5. Cook 20 minutes
6. Use slow release method

Pressure Cooker Pork Chops & Potatoes

Ingredients:

- 6 pork chops

- ½ cup beef broth

- 1 clove garlic minced

- 1 tsp salt

- ½ tsp pepper

- 1 tbs olive oil

- 15 baby red potatoes washed

Directions:

1. Put olive oil in cooker and turn on high

2. Add broth, pork chops and potatoes, cook on high 7 minutes

3. Add garlic, salt and pepper

4. Cook on high 20 minutes

5. Use slow release method

6. Serve broth as au jus sauce

Pressure Cooker Black Bean Soup

Ingredients:

- 1 Pound black beans (approx. 2-1/2 cups)
- 5 cups chicken broth
- 2 cups water
- 1-1/2 cup corn
- 1 onion chopped
- 3 potatoes peeled washed and cubed
- 1 bay leaf
- 2 cloves garlic, minced
- 1 tsp salt
- ½ tsp pepper
- 2 carrots peeled and chopped

Directions:

1. Turn cooker to high and add ¼ cup of broth
2. Pour beans in and cook on high 5 minutes
3. Add remaining broth, and water
4. Add onion, potatoes, corn, and carrots

5. Add garlic, salt, and pepper

6. Turn cooker to medium, and cook 30 minutes

7. Use slow release method

8. Stir carefully and serve

Pressure Cooker Potato Ham Casserole

Ingredients:

- 5 russet potatoes, peeled and cubed
- 2 pounds lean ham cubed
- 2 cups peas & carrots mixed vegetables
- 1 onion chopped
- 2 cloves garlic minced
- 2 tbs olive oil
- 2 cups chicken broth
- 1 tsp salt
- ½ tsp pepper
- ½ cup shredded cheese

Directions:

1. Put olive oil in cooker, add potatoes and cook 5 minutes
2. Add onion and garlic
3. Add chicken broth
4. Add ham and peas/carrots

5. Sprinkle with salt and pepper

6. Cook on high 20 minutes

7. Release using slow release method

8. Put in serving dish and sprinkle with cheese

Pressure Cooker Cilantro Chicken

Ingredients:

- 3 boneless skinless chicken breasts
- 1 tbs olive oil
- ½ cup cilantro chopped
- ½ onion chopped
- 12 ounce can green salsa
- ¾ cup chicken broth
- ½ cup shredded cheese

Directions:

1. Put oil in cooker and add chicken
2. Cook 5 minutes and add cilantro
3. Add onion, salsa and chicken broth
4. Cook on high 20 minutes
5. Use quick release method
6. Sprinkle with cheese

Pressure Cooker Marinated Grilled Shrimp

Ingredients:

- 2 pounds peeled shrimp
- ½ cup olive oil
- ½ cup tomato sauce
- ½ onion chopped
- ½ cup cooking sherry
- ¾ cup water

Directions:

1. Put oil in cooker add shrimp
2. Add tomato sauce, cooking sherry, and water
3. Add water and onion
4. Cook on high 15 minutes
5. Use quick release method

Potato Skillet Dinner

Ingredients:

- 1-3 to 3-1/2 pound round steak cut into strips
- 3 russet potatoes cut into strips
- 2 bell peppers, chopped
- 3 tbs olive oil
- I onion chopped
- 2 cloves garlic minced
- ½ cup beef broth
- 1 tsp salt
- ½ tsp pepper

Directions:

1. Add oil to cooker and turn on high
2. Add meat, onion, and potatoes, cook for 5 minutes
3. Add peppers and garlic
4. Add broth, salt, and pepper
5. Cook on high 20 minutes
6. Use slow release method

7. Stir when done

Apple Pork with Corn

Ingredients:

- Pork loin – about 3 pounds
- ½ cup apple jelly
- 1 tbs butter
- 2 cups corn kernels
- 1 apple peeled and cubed
- ½ cup beef broth
- ½ cup apple juice

Directions:

1. Put butter in cooker, add pork and cook 10 minutes on high
2. Spread jelly on pork
3. Add corn and apple
4. Pour in broth and juice
5. Cook on high 15 minutes
6. Use slow release method

Beef Nachos

Ingredients:

- 2 pounds lean ground beef
- 1 8 ounces jar taco sauce
- ½ cup salsa
- 1 onion chopped fine
- Nacho chips
- ½ cup shredded cheese

Directions:

1. Put beef in cooker, turn to high and cook 5 minutes crumble meat
2. Add taco sauce and salsa
3. Add onion and stir
4. Cook on high 15 minutes
5. Use slow release method
6. Spoon mixture over nacho chips, sprinkle with cheese

Salmon Almandine

Ingredients:

- 2 pounds fresh salmon
- ¾ cup slivered almonds
- 1 tbs olive oil
- 1 clove garlic
- 1 tsp salt
- 1 tsp white pepper
- ½ cup lemon juice
- parmesan cheese

Directions:

1. Add oil to cooker
2. Put salmon in pot and cook on high 3 minutes
3. Add almonds and garlic
4. Add salt, pepper, and juice
5. Cook on high 20 minutes
6. Use quick release method
7. Sprinkle with Parmesan

Lemon Pepper Chicken

Ingredients:

- 3 pounds chicken thighs
- ¾ cup lemon juice
- 1 tsp white pepper
- 1 tsp Lemmon pepper
- 1 tsp salt
- 1 yellow bell pepper

Directions:

1. Put chicken in pot and cook on high 5 minutes
2. Sprinkle with pepper, salt, and lemon pepper
3. Add juice and bell pepper
4. Cook on high 20 minutes
5. Use slow release method

Meatloaf Casserole

Ingredients:

- 1-1/2 pounds lean ground beef
- 1 cup Italian bread crumbs
- 1 tsp Worcestershire sauce
- 1 can stewed tomatoes
- ½ cup chicken broth
- 1 egg beaten
- ½ cup Heinz 57 sauce

Directions:

1. Add beef to cook, crumble and cook on high 5 minutes
2. Add broth, egg, Worcestershire
3. Add tomatoes and bread crumbs
4. Stir and cook on high 15 minutes
5. Use slow release method

Turkey Casserole

Ingredients:

- 24-ounce package whole wheat pasta
- 2 pounds ground turkey
- 4 cups spinach leaves chopped
- 2 cups reduced fat Alfredo sauce (available in jars or in dairy case)
- 1-1/2 cups tomatoes, chopped
- 1 tsp oregano
- 1 tsp salt
- ½ tsp pepper
- Parmesan cheese - sprinkle

Directions:

1. Add turkey to cooker and cook on high 5 minutes
2. Add spinach, Alfredo, and tomatoes
3. Add pasta
4. Add seasonings
5. Cook on high 20 minutes
6. Use slow release method

Stew Chicken& Rice

Ingredients:

- 3 pounds chicken thighs
- 1 cup brown rice
- 1 tsp pepper
- 1 tsp salt
- 1 green bell pepper
- 3 cups chicken broth
- 1 cup chopped carrots

Directions:

1. Put chicken in pot and cook on high 5 minutes
2. Sprinkle with pepper and salt
3. Add broth and rice
4. Add carrots and pepper
5. Cook on high 20 minutes
6. Use slow release method

Tomato Soup

Ingredients:

- 3 cans stewed tomatoes
- 2 cups tomato juice
- 1 tsp salt
- ½ tsp pepper
- 1 tsp oregano

Directions:

1. Put juice and tomatoes in cooker turn to high
2. Add salt, pepper, and oregano
3. Cook on high 15 minutes
4. Use slow release method
5. Use potato masher and mash all ingredients to make soup

Honey Ham

Ingredients:

- 3 pounds boneless ham
- ½ cup honey
- 2 tbs brown mustard
- 3 tbs cloves, crushed
- ¼ cup water
- 3 tbs butter

Directions:

1. Add ham to cooker
2. Pour honey over ham
3. Add butter and mustard
4. Add cloves to bottom of cooker
5. Add water
6. Cook on high 20 minutes
7. Use slow release method

Pressure Cooker Brown Rice & Peppers

Ingredients:

- 2 cups brown rice

- 1 cup chicken broth

- 1-3/4 cup water

- 1 tsp. salt (optional)

- 1 green bell pepper finely chopped

- 1 red bell pepper finely chopped

- 1 yellow bell pepper finely chopped

- 1 tbs. olive oil

Directions:

1. Heat olive oil in bottom of pressure cooker 3 minutes

2. Add rice and stir about 1 minute

3. Pour in water & chicken broth

4. Sprinkle with salt (optional)

5. Add all 3 peppers and stir lightly

6. Lock lid and set timer for 25 minutes

7. When timer beeps, use natural pressure release for 10 minutes, then quick pressure release

8. When valve drops, slowly remove lid

9. Using a fork, stir lightly until peppers are mixed well with rice, and rice appears fluffy

Pressure Cooker Italian Jambalaya

Ingredients:

- 1 tbs. olive oil
- 1 pound no yolks (or your favorite) pasta
- 2 tbs. concentrated tomato paste
- ½ tsp. salt
- cups water
- 1 cup broccoli
- 1 pound turkey sausage
- 1 clove garlic, minced finely

Directions:

1. Add oil to pressure cooker and heat for 2 minutes
2. Stir in sausage and crumble as it cooks for 5 minutes
3. Add pasta and water
4. Stir in tomato paste and add salt
5. Place broccoli evenly on top of pasta
6. Distribute pasta in pot & add enough of the water to cover the top of pasta

7. Turn pressure to high, and when it indicates low pressure, reduce pressure to medium and cook 7 minutes

8. Using natural release method for 10 minutes, and slowly remove pasta mixture into service dish and sprinkle with garlic

Pressure Cooker Turkey Chili

Ingredients:

- 1 tbs olive oil

- 1 pound turkey

- 1 16 ounces can tomato sauce

- ½ tsp. Salt

- 1 small onion

- 1 green bell pepper chopped

- 1-1/2 cup water (approx)

- 1 pack chili seasoning mix

Directions:

1. Pour olive oil into the cooker and add turkey.

2. Cook while breaking turkey up, about 4 minutes, or until brown

3. Add tomato sauce and salt.

4. Stir in onion and pepper, add chili pack and stir

5. Add just enough water to cover ingredients and set timer for

6. 20 minutes on high. When timer beeps use natural release method.

Pressure Cooker Chicken & Noodles

Ingredients:

- 2 tsps olive oil
- 1 medium onion chopped finely
- 2 medium carrots chopped
- 3 celery stalks diced
- 3 boneless, skinless chicken breasts
- 3 boneless, skinless chicken thighs
- ½ tsp. kosher salt
- ½ tsp. white pepper (black is fine also)
- 1 cup frozen peas
- 5 cups chicken broth
- 1-1/2 cups egg noodles

Directions:

1. Put olive oil into the cooker and add onions, carrots & celery. Cook 5 minutes
2. Add frozen peas and mix, sprinkle with salt and pepper
3. Add chicken breasts and thighs, and egg noodles

4. Add broth to cover contents, and set pot to 25 minutes on high

5. When timers beeps, use quick release method, when safe to open, stir

Pressure Cooker Chicken Salad

Ingredients:

- 2 tsps olive oil

- small onion, chopped

- 1 red bell pepper chopped

- 1 cucumber chopped

- boneless, skinless chicken breasts

- Slivered almonds

- ½ tsp. kosher salt

- ½ ground pepper

- 1 cup chicken broth

- ½ cup water (approx)

- 1 carton Greek yogurt, plain

Directions:

1. Pour oil into cooker and add onion, sauté until translucent

2. Add bell pepper and slivered almonds, sprinkle with salt & pepper

3. Add cucumber and chicken, cover contents with broth

4. Add water just to ensure ingredients are covered

5. Set cooker to high and cook 20 minutes

6. When timer beeps, use quick release method

7. Allow to cool, then transfer to bowl

8. Mix in yogurt and refrigerate until cool

Pressure Cooker Stuffed Potatoes

Ingredients:

- 2 tsps olive oil

- 1 cup lean ham pieces chopped into squares

- ½ cup light sour cream

- 4 tsps butter or margarine

- ½ cup shredded cheese (any kind is fine)

- 4 large baking potatoes

- 2 cups water (approx)

Directions:

1. Pour olive oil in cooker and heat on high

2. Wash potatoes well and pierce each on with fork

3. Place potatoes in cooker, and cover with water to top of potatoes

4. Set cooker for 15 minutes on high (if you prefer softer potatoes cook for 20 minutes)

5. When timer beeps, use natural release method

6. Remove potatoes and slice each potato down the center

7. Place a tsp butter, sour and sour cream in each potato and sprinkle with salt and pepper

8. Put ham pieces and cheese in potatoes and return to cooker

9. Set timer for 5 minutes and use quick release method

Pressure Cooker Chicken Vegetable Medley

Ingredients:

- 2 tsps olive oil

- 3 boneless skinless chicken breasts, cut into thin strips

- 2 cups whole kernel corn

- 1-1/2 cups chopped carrots

- 2 cups green peas

- 1 green bell pepper

- 2 cups fat-free chicken broth (approx)

- 1 tsp salt

- 1 clove chopped garlic (optional)

- ½ tsp ground pepper

Directions:

1. Heat olive oil in cooker, and add chicken strips

2. Add corn, carrots, peas and bell pepper

3. Add chopped garlic, salt, and pepper

4. Pour chicken broth, just to the top of contents

5. Set cooker to high and cook 20 minutes

6. Release using natural method

7. Put in serving dish and stir

Pressure Cooker Steak Burrito's

Ingredients:

- 2 tsps olive oil

- 1 pound lean round steak cut into thin strips

- 1 red bell pepper chopped finely

- 1 green bell pepper chopped finely

- 1 yellow bell pepper chopped finely

- 1 medium onion chopped finely

- 1 can black beans

- 6 flour tortillas

- ¾ cup salsa

- ½ shredded mozzarella cheese

Directions:

1. Heat olive oil and add onion to cooker, cook on high for 2 minutes until translucent, add all chopped pepper

2. Add meat slices and black beans, stir slightly

3. Add enough water to cover contents

4. Cook on high for 15 minutes, and use quick release method

5. Spoon mixture into flour tortillas, and add cheese

6. Fold bottom of the tortilla, then sides to create a fold that will keep meat mixture in place.

7. Top with salsa & serve

Pressure Cooker Turkey Wraps

Ingredients:

- 1 tbs olive oil

- small onion, cut into quarters

- 1 can (14 ounces) fat-free chicken stock

- 6 tortilla wraps, flour

- cartons plain Greek yogurt (can substitute ¾ cup mayonnaise)

- 1 3-5 pound turkey breast

- Dash of salt

- Dash of pepper

Directions:

1. Pour olive oil in cooker and heat up

2. Salt and pepper turkey and place in cooker

3. Layer onion quarters on turkey

4. Add salt and pepper

5. Pour in chicken stock and cook on high 25 minutes

6. When the timer beeps, use quick release method.

7. When cooled, remove turkey and shred

8. Place shredded turkey in bowl and mix in yogurt

9. Place turkey mixture into 6 flour tortillas and wrap

Pressure Cooker Garlic Potatoes with Ham

Ingredients:

- 2 pounds potatoes (russet is best) peeled and washed, and cut into cubes

- 3 large cloves of garlic

- 2 tsp butter or margarine

- 2 cups chicken broth

- 1 cup pre-cooked ham, cut into cubes

- 1 tsp kosher salt

- Dash of pepper, to taste

Directions:

1. Place potatoes, garlic, and chicken broth in cooker

2. Set cooker to high and cook 5 minutes

3. Use quick release method when timer beeps, leave in pot

4. Add butter, salt and pepper

5. Mash potatoes and garlic using masher or mixer

6. Add cubed ham & mix in

7. Serve warm

Pressure Cooker Lemon Rice with Shrimp

Ingredients:

- 1 cup long grain rice

- 2 tsp lemon juice

- ½ tsp lemon rind (or peel)

- 1 cup peeled shrimp

- 1 cup chicken broth

- 2 cups water

- ½ tsp salt

Directions:

1. Place rice, chicken broth, salt and lemon juice in metal bowl that fits in cooker, stir slightly

2. Add shrimp and mix in lightly

3. Cover top of bowl tightly with the aluminum foil

4. Add water to pot

5. Place bowl into pot, and cook on high for 5 minutes

6. Use slow release method

7. Remove bowl and stir to mix

Pressure Cooker Wild Rice Fruit & Nut Medley

Ingredients:

- 1 tbs olive oil

- 1 medium onion finely chopped

- 1-3/4 cups wild rice

- 2-1/4 cups beef broth

- 2 cups water

- 1 cup raisins

- ½ cup water chestnuts (can substitute almonds or pecans)

Directions:

1. Turn cooker on to medium, and sauté onion about 1 – 2 minutes

2. In a metal bowl that will fit in cooker, combine onion with rice and beef broth

3. Cover bowl tightly with aluminum and place in cooker

4. Pour in water and cook on high 10 minutes

5. Use natural release method

6. Add raisins and stir

7. Add chestnuts and stir

Instant Pot Meatballs and Sauce

Ingredients:

- 1 pound bag, pre-cooked frozen meatballs
- 2 tbls olive oil

Sauce:

- 2 cups chicken stock or broth
- ¾ cup tomato sauce
- ½ cup tomato paste
- 2 tsp Italian seasoning (or oregano)

Directions:

1. Mix sauce ingredients in and put in cooker, cook sauce 5 minutes on high
2. Use quick release method
3. Add frozen meatballs
4. Add olive oil and cook on high 10 minutes
5. Use slow release method
6. Place in servicing dish and sprinkle with Parmesan cheese

Pressure Cooker Chicken Enchiladas

Ingredients:

- 3 boneless skinless chicken breasts, cut into strips
- 1 tsp olive oil
- 1 small onion chopped
- 2 10.5 ounces cans enchilada sauce
- 1 cup shredded cheese (Mexican cheese works best)
- 6 flour tortillas

Directions:

1. Use metal bowl that fits in cooker
2. Put olive oil in bowl
3. Put chicken strips in and add onion, stir
4. Pour in cans of enchilada sauce and stir
5. Place bowl in cooker and turn to high
6. Cook 15 minutes and use slow release method
7. Remove bowl, and stir mixture
8. Spoon into tortillas, add cheese and fold

Pressure Cooker Vegetable Soup

Ingredients:

- 1 can stew tomatoes
- 1 can whole kernel corn
- 1 can cut green beans
- 1 can Lima beans
- 2 cups beef broth
- 1 cup chicken broth
- 1 tsp salt
- 1 tsp white pepper

Directions:

1. Put all canned vegetables into cooker
2. Add salt and pepper
3. Pour in beef broth and chicken broth
4. Set cooker to high for 15 minutes
5. Use slow release method
6. Pour into serving dishes

Pressure Cooker BBQ Corn Casserole

Ingredients:

- 1 pound lean pork, (chops or other) cut into strips (no bones)

- 1 cup BBQ sauce

- 1 can whole kernel corn

- 1 10.5 ounces can cream of mushroom soup

- 1 tsp salt

- 1 tsp pepper

- 1 medium onion chopped

Directions:

1. Put pork strips in cooker and heat

2. Add salt and pepper

3. Pour in BBQ sauce, and soup, stir

4. Add onion

5. Heat on high 15 minutes

6. Use slow release method

Pressure Cooker Broccoli Cheese Casserole

Ingredients:

- 1 10.5 ounces can cream of mushroom soup

- 1 cup Greek yogurt

- 1 egg slightly beaten

- 3 10 ounces packages frozen broccoli

- 6 ounces shredded mozzarella cheese

- Dash salt and pepper

Directions:

1. Use metal bowl that fits in cooker

2. Place soup and yogurt in bowl, stir

3. Add egg, mix in

4. Add broccoli, and sprinkle with salt and pepper

5. Cook on high 15 minutes

6. Use slow release method & serve

Pressure Cooker Italian Chicken Soup

Ingredients:

- 2 tsp olive oil
- ½ pound turkey sausage
- 1 large onion chopped
- 2 cloves garlic minced
- 1 cup spinach leaves chopped
- 3 boneless skinless chicken breasts, chopped
- 1/3 cup parsley flakes
- 1 15 ounces can chickpeas
- 1 cup medium salsa
- 3-1/2 cups chicken broth or stock

Directions:

1. Add oil ice oil and heat in cooker
2. Place sausage and chicken in and heat 2 minutes
3. Add onion, garlic, spinach leaves, chickpeas and parsley flakes
4. Add in salsa and stir

5. Pour in chicken broth/stock and stir lightly

6. Cook on high for 20 minutes

7. Use slow release method

Pressure Cooker Egg Salad

Ingredients:

- 7 large eggs

- 2/3 cup light mayonnaise

- ¼ cup spicy mustard

- 1/3 cup sweet relish

- Bread for sandwiches

Directions:

1. Place eggs in steamer basket and place in cooker

2. Add enough water to cover eggs

3. Turn cooker to high for 5 minutes

4. Release slow method, as cooker is cooling, mix mayonnaise, mustard, and relish

5. Remove eggs and place in bowl of ice water for 45 seconds

6. Remove eggs and peel

7. Chop eggs and add to mixture

Pressure Cooker Taco Casserole

Ingredients:

- 1 lb. extra lean ground beef
- 1 cup long grain rice
- 1 can (or 1-1/2 cup) stewed tomatoes
- 1 packet (or to taste) taco seasoning)
- 8 taco shells
- ¾ cup shredded cheese
- ¾ cup water
- 1 cup tortilla chips

Directions:

1. Put ground beef in metal bowl to fit in cooker
2. Heat in cooker 3 minutes
3. Add water, and rice, stir
4. Add tomatoes and taco seasoning, stir
5. Cook on high 15 minutes

6. Release using natural method

7. Layer cooked ingredients with chips and sprinkle with cheese

Pressure Cooker Corn Soufflé

Ingredients:

- 4 large eggs

- 1 can whole kernel corn

- 1 can cream style corn

- ½ cup milk

- ¼ cup sugar

- 3 tbs flour

- salt & pepper to taste

Directions:

1. Beat eggs with milk and pour into bowl that fits in cooker

2. Add cans of corn and stir slightly

3. Add sugar, salt, and pepper

4. Add flour and stir

5. Add steamer basket to cooker

6. Place pan with contents into cooker with basket and cook on high 10 minutes

7. Release using quick release method

Pressure Cooker Tomato Soup

Ingredients:

- 2 cups fresh tomatoes, chopped

- 1 small or ½ large onion, chopped

- 2 tbs olive oil

- 2 tbs flour

- 1-2 teaspoons salt (according to taste)

- 1 tsp salt

- 1 tsp pepper

- 1 tsp oregano

Directions:

1. Place onion in bowl that fits in cooker and adds olive oil, cook on high 2 minutes

2. Add tomatoes, beef broth, salt, pepper, and oregano

3. With bowl in cooker, turn cooker to high and cook for 15 minutes

4. Release quick release method, add flour and stir until smooth

Pressure Cooker Chicken Tortellini Soup

Ingredients:

- 1 14.5 ounces can chicken broth

- 1 lb chicken breasts, cut into small pieces

- 1 12 ounces package tortellini with cheese

- 2 cans chicken & herb cream soup

- 2 cups milk (approx.)

- 1 12 ounces package chopped spinach, cut

- 1 tsp salt

- ¼ tsp pepper

Directions:

1. Place chicken in cooker and turn to high

2. Add chicken broth, and soups

3. Add tortellini shells, spinach, salt & pepper

4. Stir, and add milk to desired consistency.

5. Cook on high 20 minutes

6. Use slow release method, stir and serve

Pressure Cooker Vegetable Stew

Ingredients:

- 4 cups beef broth
- 2 14.5 ounces cans stewed tomatoes
- 2 large potatoes, cut into Cubes
- 1 cup Lima beans
- 1 green bell pepper chopped
- 1 red bell pepper chopped
- 1 large onion chopped
- 1 medium carrots, peeled and chopped
- Salt & pepper to taste

Directions:

1. Pour broth into cooker, turn on high
2. Add tomatoes, potatoes, Lima beans, peppers, onion, and carrots
3. Add salt & pepper and turn cooker to high
4. Cook 20 minutes and use slow release method
5. Pour in serving dishes, garnish with cheese if desired

Pressure Cooker Cheese Steak Casserole

Ingredients:

- 2 tbs, olive oil
- 1 pound round or flank steak, sliced very thin
- 1 large onion, cut into strips
- 1 green bell pepper cut into strips
- ¾ cup shredded provolone cheese
- 4 pita pockets (or other similar bread)

Directions:

1. Pour olive oil into cooker, turn on high
2. Add steak and onions, cook for 3 minutes
3. Add peppers, and cook on high 10 minutes
4. Use fast release method
5. Layer mixture into pita pockets or onto bread, sprinkle with provolone cheese

Pressure Cooker Chicken Mushroom Casserole

Ingredients:

- 2 tbs, olive oil
- 3 boneless skinless chicken breast cut into pieces
- 8-10 button mushrooms, washed and cut in half
- 2 cans cream of mushroom soup
- 1 14.5 ounces can chicken broth
- 2 medium carrots, peeled and chopped
- 1 medium onion, chopped
- 1 cup brown rice

Directions:

1. Put olive oil in cooker, turn to high
2. Add chicken, onions and peppers
3. Add carrots, pour in broth and soups
4. Add rice, mushrooms, and carrots
5. Turn cooker to high and cook 20 minutes
6. Use slow release method

7. Serve hot

Pressure Cooker Mexican Skillet Dinner

Ingredients:

- 1 tbs, olive oil

- 1 lb. extra lean ground beef

- 2 cups long grain rice

- 1 14.5 ounces can black beans

- 1 large jar salsa

- 1 medium onion chopped

- ¾ cup shredded taco cheese

Directions:

1. Use pan suitable to fit in cooker

2. Pour olive oil into pan and place in cooker

3. Add ground beef and onion, cook 3 minutes on high

4. Add salsa and beans, stir slightly

5. Add rice and stir

6. Cook on high 15 minutes

7. Use quick release method

8. Put in serving dish and sprinkle with cheese

Pressure Cooker Chicken & Dumplings

Ingredients:

- 1 tbs, olive oil
- 3 boneless skinless chicken wings cut into pieces
- 2 cups chicken broth
- 2 10.5 ounces cans fat-free cream of chicken soup
- 1 can biscuits
- 1 tsp salt
- ½ tsp pepper

Directions:

1. Place oil in cooker, add chicken
2. Cook chicken 5 minutes
3. Add chicken broth
4. Pull biscuits apart into pieces, about 4-5 per biscuit
5. Put biscuit pieces in pot
6. Add soups, salt and pepper
7. Cook on high 15 minutes

8. Use quick release method

9. Stir, and put in serving bowls

Pressure Cooker Boneless Chicken Wings

Ingredients:

- 2 tbs, olive oil

- 3 boneless skinless chicken wings cut into cubes

- ¼ cup honey

- ½ cup hot sauce (or flavor of your choice)

- ½ cup chicken broth

- ½ cup flour

Directions:

1. Use pan suitable to fit in cooker

2. Pour olive oil into pan and place in cooker

3. Roll chicken pieces in flour, shake off excess

4. Add chicken to cooker and cook 5 minutes

5. Mix broth, honey, and hot sauce, pour over chicken

6. Cook on high 15 minutes

7. Use quick release method

8. Put in serving dish and serve with celery and dressing

Pressure Cooker Pumpkin Soup

Ingredients:

- 2 cups canned pumpkin
- 1 cup milk
- 4 cups chicken broth
- 1 cup applesauce
- 1 cinnamon stick
- 1 tsp nutmeg
- 1 tsp ginger
- 1 tsp salt
- ½ tsp pepper
- 1 large Apple, peeled and cut into cubes

Directions:

1. Put pumpkin in cooker, add milk
2. Pour in chicken broth, applesauce, and apple chunks
3. Add salt, pepper, and butter
4. Add ginger and nutmeg, stir
5. Cook on high for 15 minutes, use slow release method

Pressure Cooker Traditional Beef Stew

Ingredients:

- 2 tbs olive oil

- 1 pound lean stew beef

- 4 cups beef broth

- 1 pack beef stew mix

- 1 tbs flour

- 2 large carrots, peeled and chopped

- 4 medium potatoes, peeled and chopped

- 2 medium onions, peeled and sliced

- 1 tsp salt

- ½ tsp pepper

Directions:

1. Put oil in cook and add meat, turn to high

2. Add potatoes and onions, stir

3. Add salt, pepper, and broth

4. Add stew mix packet and flour, stir until mixed

5. Add remaining ingredients and cook on high 20 minutes

6. Use slow release method

Pressure Cooker Garlic Roasted Potatoes & Ham

Ingredients:

- 2 tbs olive oil

- 8 small red potatoes, washed well

- 4 cups chicken broth

- 2 cloves garlic, minced

- 1 so thyme

- 1 tbs butter

- 1 cup lean ham, cut into cubes

- 1 medium onion finely chopped

- 1 tsp salt

- ½ tsp pepper

Directions:

1. Put oil in cooker, and potatoes and stir

2. Add onion and garlic, mix in

3. Add salt, pepper, thyme and butter

4. Cook on high for 20 minute

5. Use slow release method, and add ham cubes

6. Stir ham in and serve warm

Pressure Cooker Lemon Herb Chicken & Rice

Ingredients:

- 2 tbs olive oil
- 3 boneless skinless chicken breasts, cut into strips
- 3 cups chicken broth
- 1 clove garlic, minced
- 1 tsp salt
- ½ tsp pepper
- ½ cup lemon juice
- ½ tsp lemon peel
- 2 cups long grain rice

Directions:

1. Put olive oil in cooker, add chicken
2. Add broth and cook on high for one minute
3. Add garlic, salt and pepper
4. Stir in lemon juice and add lemon peel
5. Add rice and cook on high 20 minutes

6. Use quick release method and serve warm

Tacos and Rice

Ingredients:

- taco shells
- 1 pound ground beef
- 1 cup rice
- 1-1/2 cup taco sauce
- ½ cup salsa
- 1 can Rotel

Directions:

1. Add beef to cooker, crumble
2. Cook on high 5 minutes
3. Add rice, taco sauce and salsa
4. Add Rotel
5. Cook on high 15 minutes
6. Use quick release method
7. Spoon mixture into taco shells

Conclusion

Congratulations for completing the book so fast. We are sure you must have had a great time reading it. Instant Pot recipes are taking the entire world by a storm. Now, with the help of this comprehensive and fun recipe book, you can certainly experiment a little and prepare nutritive meals for you and your loved ones.

We have covered recipes of various kinds. From soups and burrito bowls to quinoa and baked dishes, the book has a diverse range of quick and easy recipes. We have provided an easy stepwise process for one to cook these meals without any trouble. You can easily cook these recipes all by yourself or can involve your loved ones in the process. After all, the more the merrier, right?

Our focus was on breakfast recipes and we tried to come up with various kinds of meals that can be cooked in the blink of an eye. Breakfast is all about being quick, but at the same time, it is also the most important meal of the day. One should never compromise on the nutritive value that they can get a breakfast.

Instant Pots and Pressure Cookers are gradually making a way in our kitchen. One of the best parts of these appliances is their quick turnaround time. There is a reason why they are called "instant" pots. One can easily prepare a meal while saving their time and without compromising on the taste of the food. Now, you can cook your favorite recipes on the go with the help of your instant pot.

Instant pots are energy efficient as well and unlike any other cooking equipment, it preserves the nutritive value of the food. We have handpicked some of the healthiest dishes for you so that you can take care of yourself and prepare these tasty recipes in no time. Don't withhold yourself and start cooking. Experiment a little and give your own signature touch to these classic recipes.

65477285R10089

Made in the USA
Charleston, SC
21 December 2016